METANOIA

METANOIA

SHARON MCCARTNEY

BIBLIOASIS
WINDSOR, ONTARIO

FIRST EDITION

Library and Archives Canada Cataloguing in Publication

McCartney, Sharon, 1959-, author
        Metanoia / Sharon McCartney.

Poem.
Issued in print and electronic formats.
ISBN 978-1-77196-068-7 (paperback).--ISBN 978-1-77196-069-4 (ebook)

        I. Title.

PS8575.C427M48 2016   C811'.54   C2015-907392-8
                                                C2015-907393-6

Edited by Zachariah Wells
Copy-edited by Emily Donaldson
Typeset by Chris Andrechek
Cover designed by Kate Hargreaves
Cover image by Jennifer McIntyre

Published with the generous assistance of the Canada Council for the Arts and the Ontario Arts Council. Biblioasis also acknowledges the support of the Government of Canada through the Canada Book Fund and the Government of Ontario through the Ontario Book Publishing Tax Credit.

PRINTED AND BOUND IN CANADA

METANOIA

Like Jesus, I was born in the desert,
the barrens under Camelback Mountain.
That emptiness has dogged me all my life,

an arid wind clawing my sundress
on the gravel playground.

I banished the banker forever.
I didn't really want to be alone, as I'd told him.
I just didn't want to be with him.

The banker said, "Great.
Being with no one is better than being with me."

Mother said, "Smile.
Learn to cook Swiss steak.
Sew a French seam.
Be a good wife."

I think, now, that she should have known better.

How I told myself that I loved
the husband more than he loved me.

I loved him so much
I wanted to be him.
I thought that was love.
He did not want to be me.
I saw that as a lack.
And left.

All of that effort to make myself loveable made me unloving.

When the married man rebuffed me, I was worthless.
In this way, I discovered my worth.

How crushed I was if he did not respond to an email.

Then furious.

I do not believe in death anymore.
For you people, perhaps. But not for me.

The man in New Mexico said maybe the secret
is to find someone with matching neuroses.
But I want him to be hot as well.

I am not alone.
I am in an exclusive relationship with myself.

I knew that the fat man was wrong,
not immediately, but soon enough.
The way he crowded me on the sidewalk.

A warm rain in the lime tree.
Pigeons fucking under the eaves.
My sad neighbour feeds them.
I wish she would not.

When I say that I do not want anyone but the husband,
I do not mean that I want the husband.
What I mean is that I do not want to want anyone else.

The banker said, "My life is a shambles."
I said, "Everyone's life is a shambles."

When the husband was younger,
I loved his broad shoulders, particularly
when they were above me.

Now that he's older, his shoulders
have gone soft, annular, sloping
tenderly under his mandarin collar.

And I love him again for being one of us.

The banker snored outrageously and twitched in his sleep.
I could not sleep beside him.
This became an issue.
That last night, I snuck off to the spare bedroom,
hoping for an hour or two.

At 5 A.M., I heard him downstairs, loading
his vehicle, the door slamming, his shoes,
angry. He tromped upstairs, perched on the edge
of the bed in the dark, saying, darkly,
"I didn't want to leave without saying goodbye."

No, I thought, you didn't want to leave without hurting me.

I pleased the banker. He didn't please me.
I withdrew myself. He was no longer pleased.

Eliot says, "To get to where you are not, you have to go
by the way in which you are not."
I want to love again.

The Mayan was the best.
No prudishness, no hesitation.

I said, "Could you please teach that
to every man on earth?"

If he had wanted me to come to Vancouver, I would have.

In pain, I locked the door, turned out the lights,
so he would return to a dark house,
myself in bed, my back to him.

All of this to push him away,
when his leaving was what I feared.

That night that I walked home in the dark, weeping.

Blue in the sky soon.
Hope would be hope for the wrong thing.

We all just want to be loved.
Which is the same as being unloved.

I strung the fat man along;
I thought I was sparing him.

A lie. I was sparing myself.

Because I waited too long to speak,
I became revulsed.

The last time we had sex, I said to myself,
"This is the last time."
I did not say that to him.

How to live then?
Honour my mother.
Honour what is in me that is her.

Be true to my loneliness.

That scares the shit out of me.

I always loved the husband. Oh when I first saw him,
six-pack slung on his back, in hiking boots.
How he flirted with me, poking my shoulder.

What I did not love was myself with him.

The task is not to find god or a new man.
The task is to find wholeness, magnitude.
Having that, all other needs fall away.

I used alcohol to mask insufficiency.
Ditto men.

Alcohol has become too complicated for me.
Ditto men.

Eliot says the ocean is us.
We cannot think of a time that is not oceanless
because it does not exist.

California resides in my memory as the occidental aroma of exhaust and brine.

Grieving the marriage,
I grieved the loss of my abode for love.
I was taught not to love myself.
A girl should accommodate.
A girl should not love herself,
or no one will like her.
This was the supreme hell. To be unliked.

I am continually struck by the oddity of the mirror.
Who is that visage? I do not feel so contained.

And there it is again, inexplicably, the fear
that I have nothing if I do not have the husband.
That is the fear I must stride toward.
Walk into it even though my stomach is upside down,
even though I would rather not.

Younger, I wanted to obliterate myself.

Older, I want to uncover myself.

What I did to the banker was unkind.

If I seek wholeness, I am entirely unwhole.
Therefore, seek emptiness.

Light snow falling.
No wind. All acute angles softened,
corners blunted, discordances resolved.

Nine years ago, mired in despair,
disillusioned, believing I had been betrayed,
I found snowbanks seductive, imagined laying myself
down in their alabaster deeps.

This was ridiculous.
Further, no one had betrayed me.

All of life is a learning to let go
until life lets go of us.

Grace is the time in which to do this.

The banker wanted me beside him all night,
no matter what.

Let the husband go to his blonde,
strumming her twelve-string.
That would have been better.
Not my dire meddling. Even my rejection
of him was grasping.

The thrill of the unknown waned and then
there was nada. The banker's tongue down my throat,
but I just wanted to watch *Friends*.

Marrying was escaping my mother,
her life of diminishment,
her colonial furniture and braided rugs,
her Tennessee Ernie Ford.
Anything but that, I said.

Break up with the banker on Sunday.
On Tuesday, a Facebook friend
request. He had unfriended me.
Then reconsidered. Just as I have done.
This almost makes me love him.

The pain is not the pain of losing the husband, of seeing him
with another, trying to please her, but a deeper,
more fundamental ache.

What was I trying to avoid?
Mother, supping alone in her enormous house.

In the dream, I wanted lights on my bicycle.
The guy at Savage's showed me that they were already there,
front and back.

The owl looping through the black willows,
backlit by the group home's spotlight.
The owl is process. I am process.

Clinging not so much to life, but to life as it is now.

I hope the owl kills some of the pigeons.

The fat man thought that he knew what I wanted.
I shied from that. It's too much to ask,
to be someone whose wants can be known.

The horse shied, not at the fence,
but at the absence of fence, where one section
was removed for repairs. The opening, the break
in the rhythm of fence, fence, fence, as startling
as any fleeing rodent
or green garbage bag
torn and flapping.

We only wake up to discrepancy.

The body is a convenience.
In order to perceive a world, we have to stand outside of it,
in the stand-alone body.

Like the dog in his crate, what first appeared a prison
becomes, with time, a refuge.
Comfortable old crate. A soft rag for a bed,
a rawhide to gnaw.

The troll at work demurred,
"We are not trying to demoralize you."
Percheron man insisted, "I am not controlling."

It was in their minds first, not mine.

That lesion on my chest may well be murderous.
Listen to it.

Coffee, cigarettes, asthma puffers, anti-depressants, cookies, pie, donuts. He could not walk past sugar.

Why did Mother hate Father so much?
I do not know. It was not spoken of.

Look for beauty in the world to find it in myself.
Look for goodness in the world to find it in myself.

A thaw, rain before dawn, syncopation
of the leaf-clotted eaves,
my morning tunes.

Always the tendency toward mortification.
Starving myself as a teenager.
Quitting the comfortable job.
Walking out of the adequate marriage.
Let all of that go.
The world is mortifying enough.

What I learned from the married man:
to love without wanting to deprive
anyone else of the beloved.
The grasping is fear,
the false conviction
that if someone else has what I want
I am diminished.

The husband and I drove to Cut Bank, Montana, on Friday nights
and drank at the Winner's Circle for hours.
There were others there. Railroad workers.
The dollar-store clerk. A woman offered to buy a round.
She dumped nickels and dimes on the counter.

I dreamt of horses swimming underwater,
myself rolling over their tumbling haunches,
incipience under the surface.

I could have loved the fat man,
but his stomach got in the way.

I loved the husband but what I loved in him
was what I wanted to love in myself.
What I thought was the death of love
was only love coming home.

All shyness, all anxiety, is an excess of self-love.

Let that go.
Nothing can touch me because I touch nothing.

The basswood is budding.
The morning dogs are unleashed.

When I told the Mayan that he made me feel like a fuck,
he said, "That makes my eyeballs burn if you feel that way."

Rubbing his eyes.

And then he left.
There was Rogers Cup tennis in HD at his sister's house.

The banker said, "I feel like an imposter."
Then he said, "I meant imposer,
not imposter."

On an operating table again, under surgical lights.
The lesion on my chest is basal cell carcinoma
if I am lucky, melanoma if I am not.

A needle goes in for the freezing and I am left alone.
I'm thinking about twelve years ago, my mastectomy.
How frightened I was, my world gone cuckoo.

I lay myself down under the globular lights
and breathed down to my heart as the anesthetist
leaned over me. When I woke up in recovery,
I could see sideways a row of beds. Nurses.

One came over and said, "You were crying.
You were crying for a long time.
When we asked you what you wanted, you said,
'I want my husband.'"

The husband's overt scorn for the hoi polloi.
What was he so afraid of?

I dreamt that a passenger jet crashed into a bay
right in front of me, the wings narrowing
as it dove, like a petrel. At the same time, nearby, a ferry
capsized and sank. I could see the faces of the people
climbing out of the sinking ferry. Wet hair.
Pulling on the railings as they climbed the sinking stairs.
Gasping. Who were those people?

Jung says what we deny inwardly
will come to us outwardly as fate.

I denied my mother.

Still a little fluish, my throat rough.

The dog skulks when I cough,
as if rebuked.

The banker was always in my face, wanting to kiss me
while I chopped onions, while we waited for the elevator.
Aggressive. Tongue. Did he think that I liked that?
I shrugged him off. I need someone who doesn't need me.

What I mean is I don't want to need anyone.

Another failed relationship,
another non-stick pan ruined.

More snow in the forecast.
This year's ploughing bill will bury me.

8 A.M., whine of an engine revving.
Ballcap's Neon has foundered in the snow.
He's got a shovel. Digs a bit, gets in and spins the wheels.

The sun comes up so late these days,
sometimes I fear it won't.

The world is a story the dog reads with his nose.
His favourite work of art is an abstract of January's
sunlight on hardwood. He lays himself down,
deeply at peace, drawn into the warmth as I am drawn
into my favourite Antoine Bittar, the perspective
walking me down an unnamed street in Gloucester,
Maine. I look up from the rain-devilled sidewalk
into the argon of an amber streetlamp.

However I got here, this is where I belong.

The woman next door says, "I am going to feed
the pigeons and no one can stop me."
She says, "This is who I am. I am very passionate about this."

She's in my driveway, shouting at me.
All I can hear is I, I, I.

My pretty friend says, "My love life sucks,"
and tips her glass of pinot back.
Drinks with a colleague before meeting me,
so she's a little hammered, all dolled up and pink cheeks.

I wish she would not separate love from the rest of her life.

The last child leaves for good
and the house is empty.
A predictable sadness but also
a wholly unexpected sense of peace,
wholeness. I am that emptiness in the house.

The husband was a way to get out of myself,
out of the emptiness. As were children.
I thought that I could fill it with other people.

Don't you hate it when Buddhists get all emptier than thou?

What I felt so many years ago in the grade 9 English classroom, how I lost my sense of membrane, of containment, my self leaching into the Bermuda lawn beyond the sliding glass door, into the eucalyptus, the succulents, the birds of paradise.

The ocean is emptiness.
The ocean is us.

Acknowledgements

Metanoia originally appeared, in a slightly different version, in the November 2014 issue of *Numéro Cinq* (http://numerocinqmagazine.com/). Sincere thanks to Douglas Glover and everyone at *Numéro Cinq*.

Acknowledgements

was originally appeared, in a slightly different version, in the _Journal_ ... issue of ... (in part)...

About the Author

Sharon McCartney is the author of *Hard Ass* (2013, Palimpsest), *For and Against* (2010, Goose Lane Editions), *The Love Song of Laura Ingalls Wilder* (2007, Nightwood Editions), *Karenin Sings the Blues* (2003, Goose Lane Editions), and *Under the Abdominal Wall* (1999, Anvil Press). Her poems have been included in the 2012 and 2013 editions of *The Best Canadian Poetry in English*. She has an MFA from the University of Iowa's Writers' Workshop and an LL.B. from the University of Victoria. In 2008, she received the Acorn-Plantos People's Prize for poetry. She lives in Fredericton, New Brunswick.